POCKET IMAGES

Llandaff

Llandaff Civic Society

NONSUCH

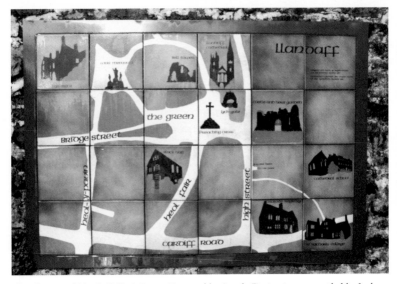

The tile map of Llandaff, High Street. Designed by Angela Davies, it was unveiled by Lady Ferguson Jones on 21 October 1981.

First published 2000
This new pocket edition 2007
Images unchanged from first edition

Nonsuch Publishing Limited
Cirencester Road, Chalford,
Stroud, Gloucestershire, GL6 8PE
www.nonsuch-publishing.com

Nonsuch Publishing is an imprint of NPI Media Group

© Llandaff Civic Society, 2000

British Library Cataloguing in Publication Data.
A catalogue record for this book is available from the British Library.

ISBN 978-1-84588-400-0

Typesetting and origination by Nonsuch Publishing Limited
Printed in Great Britain by Oaklands Book Services Limited

Contents

Above and below: Llandaff from the air, November 1999.

Preface

'Walk about Sion and go round about her: and tell the towers thereof.
Mark well her bulwarks, set up her houses: that ye may tell them that come after.'
Psalm 48 vv 11-12

There are not so many towers in Llandaff, perhaps. The tower on Insole Court, the two cathedral towers and the campanile and the little turret house in Chapel Street. You can see a fine line in bulwarks, though, if you enter Court Lane from High Street and look to your left along the magnificent thirteenth-century wall of the old Bishop's Castle. Perhaps the corner towers of the castle and the gatehouse as well, qualify for the count. And what about the houses? What a variety in size, age and style is to be found everywhere in our area of interest.

In 1993 someone suggested that a stocktaking, a sort of Llandaff Domesday Book, should be completed by the year 2000. This was, in fact, the second impulse we had had to record the Llandaff we knew. A living community changes, not always for the better, and important buildings were being lost. The imminence of the millennium sharpened our resolution.

The archive on which this book is based was compiled by members of the Llandaff Civic Society over seven years and will eventually be lodged at the Glamorgan Record Office, Cardiff. Its core is a photographic record of every building in our area and of the life of the community, some 3,000 pictures, and the 1,395 completed copies of a questionnaire which went to every household in the Ward. In addition, regular observations of birds made at fifty-nine different locations in the year 1997-98 and an updated and extended plant survey complete the picture.

It took five years of consultation and experimentation before the final version of the questionnaire was ready for delivery, and even then, with hindsight, we would have done some things differently. In English and Welsh we asked all sorts of questions compatible with, but supplementary to, the national census and other records held by the local authority. Some related to the fabric and age of the dwelling, but many were personal, and for this reason all the completed questionnaires will be embargoed for a hundred years and only statistical information will be published. After 2099, however, a student would be able to gain a vivid picture of life here at the end of the twentieth century: what brought people to Llandaff, what sort of education, jobs and recreations they had, their favourite meals, whether they kept pets, if they were on the internet, how many cars they had, whether they attended a place of worship and, most interesting, perhaps, what they liked and disliked about Llandaff. We are enormously grateful for the good temper with which so many people responded to our questions and we hope that this taster for the main archive will be of interest even more widely.

Lisbeth David
Chairman, Llandaff Civic Society

Cardiff.

With love & best wishes for a happy birthday

The City Cross, Llandaff.

Above and below: These two photographs of the Preaching Cross on the Cathedral Green are separated in time by almost one hundred years. Tower House to the left in the upper picture was swept away in the 1920s; White House, in the background, was so severely damaged by the landmine which exploded just behind it that it needed almost complete rebuilding after the war, whilst its front wall was lowered in the 1980s. The upper section of the Cross has been turned through ninety degrees and modes of transport are somewhat different. The London Plane tree lives on!

Introduction

The end of a century seems an appropriate moment to pause and to try and capture for the future a glimpse of the life of our community. The promise of a new millennium makes us all the more conscious of this landmark in history.

The Llandaff Civic Society, which has bravely taken on this task, is to be warmly congratulated on trying to look objectively at aspects of our everyday lives. Llandaff is in many ways a fascinating place, though strangers driving through will probably be too intent upon negotiating busy traffic to notice anything more than an ordinary Cardiff suburb. But Llandaff is more than a suburb; its long history has engendered a distinct sense of place. It is also many-layered, representing different things to different people.

There is 'the village', with its busy, often congested High Street leading to a comparatively tranquil and charming Green. There is a thriving ecclesiastical community centred around the cathedral itself but also including the Cathedral School and St Michael's Theological College. Education has long played a major role in the community and from primary to post-graduate level the needs of many are locally addressed. For people beyond Cardiff, Llandaff is associated with broadcasting, as for over thirty years BBC Wales has made its home here.

These are but a few of the different activities associated with Llandaff; it is a place to worship, to learn, to shop, or merely to spend an evening in the restaurant or pub. Most importantly though, Llandaff is a good place to live.

A century ago it was described as a place 'for the money-getting people' of Cardiff. The grounds of their large mansions now provide homes for the many. Even the most modest 'artisan dwellings', provided they are 'in the village', have undergone a radical gentrification. Despite pasture giving way to tarmac, Llandaff remains a green place, with a surprising variety of wildlife found in parkland and back garden.

Just as the Llandaff of 2000 is a very different place from that of 1900, so the new century will surely bring change at a frightening pace. Progress has both blessings and curses, and no doubt the images in this book will one day evoke the same nostalgia as may be found in the following 'Then and Now' pictures.

Unfortunately, there was no Llandaff Civic Society around in 1900 to capture the contemporary scene, but I imagine future historians will share our enthusiasm and even our affection for Llandaff as it experiences the third millennium.

Matthew Williams
Keeper of the Collections, Cardiff Castle
'Chalcott', Llandaff, 1999

Above and below: During the First World War 'The Lodge' was used for a time to house convalescent officers, here seen enjoying the sun and peace of Cardiff Road. Today the constant heavy traffic makes this a well-nigh impossible dream.

Below and right: Masons' tools may be much the same, but there have been many changes in working practices since the top photograph was taken on the roof of the cathedral's Jasper Tower in the 1920s, not least in protective clothing and scaffolding systems. The lower picture was taken during repair work on the Jasper Tower in 1997 and shows a stone mason carving a replacement block in the corona.

Above and below: This view across High Street from outside the NatWest Bank is in total contrast to a photograph, taken in 1867 from the same spot, of the newly completed school building which had been designed by John Prichard. This school had replaced an earlier building in High Street which now serves as the Llandaff Institute. Prichard's school was itself superseded by the present building in Hendre Close in 1967.

'Hands together, eyes closed'. *Above:* The headteacher, Mr Fred Penhallarick, conducts assembly in the hall of the old National School in the High Street, then nearing its centenary. *Below:* A generation later a class is shepherded into the school hall by teacher's aide, Mrs Heather Fry, in City of Llandaff Primary School in Hendre Close. All the pupils are in uniform and the 'ethnic mix' has begun. The wooden desks, with their ink-wells, are a thing of the past and these children sit on the polished floor. A cake stands ready to celebrate a 'Birthday Assembly'.

Above and below: It can be seen from the comparison of these two pictures, taken nearly a hundred years apart, that while the south-east side of the High Street has changed comparatively little, the north-west side has been transformed by the building of three successive terraces of shops, the last replacing the Prichard School. The bus route has changed and, of course, the bus.

Above and below: Forty years ago there was no bank in the High Street and the Maltster's Arms in Cardiff Road facing the High Street was waiting to be totally rebuilt. But Cyril Davies, of Llandaff Radio & Television (the shop on the right of both pictures) would probably agree that the greatest change since the 1950s has been the amount of traffic. Ten years ago, when asked if they would support a partial one-way system in the High Street, there was almost complete opposition from shop owners. Today, there has been a considerable swing towards the idea and a few even favour pedestrianizing the High Street.

Above and below: Howell's School hockey team, 1890, and Howell's School hockey team, 1999. Below, left to right, back row are: Alex Galanopoulos, Emma Toombs, Jenny Bland, Hannah Ward, Anjuli Davies. Middle row: Rebecca Pickering, Charlotte Howell-Richardson, Bethan Fisher (captain), Jessica Rees. Front row: Leah Barrett, Ena Culverwell, Emily Gray, Sarah Winstanley. The playing of hockey is, apparently, on the decline. There used to be four pitches in Llandaff Fields for this sport but now there is only one. Will the twenty-first century see a revival?

Above and below: Ewan Christian's Deanery, built in 1863, is now in secular occupation. The beeches of Dean's Wood, in summer at least, completely hide what is now known as 'Cathedral Court', and the mill stream, its bridge visible below the notice, is now dry and its bed overgrown with elder, alder and Japanese knotweed.

Above and below: The crowd is kept at a respectful distance as King George V and Queen Mary walk through Llandaff on their Coronation tour in 1912. They have come from the Palace (now the Cathedral School) and out through the medieval gateway of the ruined Bishop's Castle. Bishop Pritchard Hughes accompanies the King and behind them Archdeacon Buckley escorts Queen Mary. Three generations and eighty-nine years later, Charles, Prince of Wales, leaves the rest of the royal party and chats with the crowd a little further down the same road.

One
Teaching and Learning

The advertising literature of most local house-agents contains the entry 'proximity to good schools' as an inducement to buy a house in Llandaff. There is indeed a variety of educational establishments in the village-city. These cater for all ages, from the private day nurseries in Cardiff Road and at the BBC, to the University of Wales Institute on Western Avenue. Just opposite this are the headquarters of the Welsh Joint Education Committee which organizes the public examination system in Wales.

The Cathedral School provides primary education for both girls and boys. Howell's School for Girls caters for pupils from reception class to sixth form. Both these private schools were established for boarders but have recently changed to accept day pupils only—an interesting comment on social and educational thinking.

There are two Church-in-Wales schools in the parish. City of Llandaff Primary School is the only English-medium primary school at the centre of Llandaff and is, in that sense, very much the 'village school'. Bishop of Llandaff High School provides secondary education for boys and girls from a wide catchment area in the diocese. There are also large comprehensive schools at Cantonian, Fairwater and at Radyr, just outside the parish boundaries but attended by some Llandaff children.

Welsh medium education is provided at Ysgol Pencae and at Ysgol Glantaf just across the river in Llandaff North.

The Theological College of St Michael and All Angels works in close collaboration with the University of Wales, Cardiff. At the other end of the theological scale, the cathedral maintains a thriving Sunday school and under the provisions of the new curriculum it offers an expanding educational programme for visiting school parties.

In the closing years of the twentieth century the government's approach to education has become increasingly doctrinaire. Teachers are weighed down by administration—assessment, STATS, reports of all kinds. As marriage breakdown and resulting family problems impinge on the life of the pupils, members of the teaching staff are increasingly drawn into social work. On the academic level there is an emphasis from early school on information technology, which is seen as essential to preparation for the modern world. In Wales there is an increasing awareness in both English and Welsh medium schools of the importance of Welsh life and culture in the education of our children. It remains to be seen what impact the National Assembly will have on our local education system.

Few areas the size of Llandaff can boast such a wealth of educational opportunities. Students throng the streets on their way from the Halls of Residence in Llantrisant Road to the various colleges. The traffic is regularly held up by groups of pupils on their way to school services in the cathedral. Teaching and learning are seen to have prominence in life in Llandaff.

Methods may vary but the concentration is the same. Conventional drawing and colouring for the very young at the Busy Bees Nursery, where Aline Burgess guides pre-schoolers Esther Biggin, Lewis Clement and Nicola Wainwright.

At City of Llandaff Primary School a computer is operated by Rhys Jenkins. The introduction of information technology alongside the familiar number charts is a feature of early schooling today.

Lower School classes at play at City of Llandaff Primary School.

'A oes heddwch? Is there peace?' Pupils enact the ceremony of the Chairing of the Bard (in this instance, Sarah Woodington) at the St David's Day Eisteddfod in the Upper School of City of Llandaff Primary.

Above: Headteacher Mrs Eleri Jones welcomes visitors to Llandaff's Welsh language primary school, Ysgol Pencae.

Opposite below: 'Sut ydych chi? How are you?', is the message of one of the 'balloons' suspended over this class at Ysgol Pencae.

Right: Two sides of life and education at Llandaff Cathedral Choir School, founded in 1880 by Dean Vaughan to provide a good general education for boy boarders while ensuring the maintenance of the daily choral services at the cathedral. It now ranks as a preparatory day school for both boys and girls. Here, the choirboys are drawn up in the Processional Way before service.

Below: Boys and girls compete in the sack race at their Sports Day, with the cathedral in the background.

Howell's School for Girls was opened in 1860 by the Howell's Trust which had been set up to administer the bequest of Thomas Howell, a merchant of the Drapers company, who in 1536 left twelve thousand ducats for dowries for 'Orphanes of good fame ... and so every year for Maydens for ever'. In Victorian times the Court of Chancery converted the dowries into schools for boarders and day girls at Denbigh and at Llandaff. Here the youngest pupils listen to a story from Mrs Julia Eager.

The Learning Resources Centre (presided over by Mrs Pat Williams) is in the older part of Howell's School but is well-equipped to cater for study up to years twelve and thirteen (the old Sixth Form).

Craft exhibits around the trophy cabinet in Bishop of Llandaff Church in Wales High School. The school, established in 1962, draws its pupils, boys and girls, from a large number of parishes.

Excitement at the St David's Day Eisteddfod in the Sports Hall at Bishop of Llandaff High School. Pupils brandish mascots as the house points are announced. The banners represent the saints after whom the school 'houses' are named.

The cross dominates contrasting styles of architecture in the quadrangle of the Theological College of St Michael and All Angels. John Prichard's house, on the right, contains the refectory, common room, and administrative offices. The block on the left consists of study bedrooms and the two buildings are linked by more modern studies and the college library.

The typical theological student of the 1990s may well be a woman at work on her computer in her study-bedroom at St Michael's. The cassock behind the door and the coffee mug on the desk are necessary adjuncts of student life in a theological college.

The portrait of the founder surveys the refectory at St Michael's. The celibate, strictly disciplined life of a Victorian men's college has given way to a more relaxed atmosphere where tutors and students, their wives and children join together for a family meal. Would Fr Johnson have approved?

A Sunday school class meets in the Prebendal House at the cathedral. Here the photographs of former Deans look down benignly on the informal grouping.

Students of the University of Wales Institute Cardiff, Western Avenue.

The Welsh Joint Education Committee advertises help for examinees at its headquarters on Western Avenue. Here the examination syllabus is devised and papers in their thousands arrive for marking. The future of many candidates is decided here and standards in education are set for the whole of Wales.

Two
Buying and Selling

It all begins in the home, of course, and like other households in the United Kingdom, residents of Llandaff regularly receive a huge amount of commercial information. Some of it comes in the post, some is pushed through letter-boxes, others tumble out of newspapers and magazines. There are incredibly cheap books for sale (both hard-back and paperback), free trials of electronic personal organizers and access to the internet, discount on car insurance, discount offers of meals at new restaurants, invitations to attend opening days of sales, suggestions as to where to spend holidays, offers to lend money at favourable rates of interest, and to put your house on the market. And then there are the irritating people who call you on the telephone to try and persuade you to invest in double glazing, refit your kitchen or order cases of fine wines. It is sometimes a relief to go out and do some positive shopping.

In the 1960s, the Ladybird Publishing Company brought out a series of 'Learning to Read' books, with, as regular characters, two improbably well-behaved children named Janet and John. One of these books concerned a shopping expedition with their mother, calling at a number of small shops—the butcher, the baker/confectioner, the grocer, the greengrocer, the toyshop—all apparently within a comfortable walking distance from their home. At the time the book came out to some it seemed a trifle nostalgic. Shopping habits were changing, and it would have been more realistic had Janet and John been driven by their mother to a supermarket where all the shopping could have been done under one roof and piled into one trolley.

But then, as now, there were families who still preferred to patronize local shops, and in fact, if Janet, John and family were living in Llandaff today, it would be possible for a local shopping expedition to be carried out which would be not dissimilar to the one in the book. There may not be as much choice as in the supermarkets, but there is an undefinable something about the small shops that makes their possible demise in the future a matter of some regret.

Above and below: 'Estate agents and restaurants! That's what the village shops have become', was the comment of a taxi-driver driving through the main street of an English village recently. And Llandaff has its share of estate agencies; restaurants too, especially if you include the pubs (all of whom serve mid-day meals) and the takeaways, but the taxi-driver's pessimistic assessment is not borne out here, not yet anyway. For instance, Llandaff has three gift shops. A hundred years ago No. 6 High Street was a butcher's shop, but it has been 'Town and Country' for the past thirty years. Garlands, further down on the other side, started as a flower and bridal wear shop, but changed to flowers and gifts a few years ago.

Above: And the third? That is in the cathedral, where the items on sale are designed (religious and secular) mainly for visitors. All those behind the counter are volunteers.

Below: Two of the four shops in the photograph—Greenberg (optician's) and Going Places (travel agency)—are not at present affected to any extent by supermarketry. To date, only one supermarket in the Cardiff area has an optician's section, and Going Places is a branch of a major and well-established travel agency. Hall's Bookshop, however, does admit to being affected and having to take care about which books to stock (and has recently revived its picture-framing service). The fourth shop, Ambience, home designers, a relative newcomer, has now made an application for a change of use to a restaurant.

Opposite above: The largest of the three general stores in Llandaff is the Spar in the High Street and it is in most respects a typical mini-market, open from eight in the morning until late evening. One popular feature is the 'Bakers Corner', serving hot snacks and whole roast chickens. A recent addition, which started in August 1999, is a home video club

Left: Special offers for holidays in Crete, Gran Canaria, Lanzarotti, and other similar locations regularly appear in the window of Going Places, but the three top holiday spots for Llandaff residents in 1999 have all been across the Atlantic—Cuba, Mexico and Florida.

Below: The trio of three-storey buildings, at the lower end of the High Street next to the Black Lion, have been shops ever since they were built a century ago. The one in the middle, Forbuoys, has, under various managements, been a newsagent's for well over fifty years. Cathedral Cleaners, on the right, has been a dry cleaning premises for twenty years, and the café, K2, for rather less.

Number 39 Cardiff Road has been the headquarters for the past six years of 'On Screen Productions', who produce video programmes, commercials, multimedia, films and special events. This neat but modest exterior hides a successful independent communications company with a growing reputation.

33

In 1871, when Edward Fishbourne arrived at Cardiff station having applied for a minor canonry at Llandaff Cathedral, he asked a cab driver to take him to the best hotel in Llandaff, and was taken to the Red Lion Inn on the Green, where he was told he would have to 'rough it'. Today he would be taken to Churchill's Hotel in Cardiff Road and there would be no roughing it (although it would be safer to book in advance). There are twenty-two comfortable rooms and thirteen Mews apartments. Built in 1860, as one of a pair of select private houses, it became the Llandaff Hotel in the 1950s, changing its name in the mid-1970s. No-one seems to know why its name was changed, but probably the new owner was a strong admirer of Sir Winston Churchill. There is a framed photograph of the great statesman in the porch and several more in the lounge bar covering various stages of his long political career, but they were put up long after the change of name. The hotel was taken over by S.A. Brain & Co., the Cardiff brewery, in 1986.

The first shop window that people see, coming to Llandaff Cathedral along Cardiff Road, contains an unusual and impressive display of church furnishings—an altar, lectern, crosses in wood, metal and stone sculptured figures and heads as well as polished headstones. A book could be written—and we hope that one will be written—about the history of the Clarke family and their connection with Llandaff Cathedral. Today, although church furnishing work is still undertaken, the present occupant of 98 Cardiff Road is a structural engineer, and this is now the main activity.

The private car park at the rear of the Maltster's Arms is for customers at the Maltster's, Stan Cottle's betting office and 'Bully's' restaurant. Stan Cottle has been providing a service for those who love to bet on the horses for thirty-five years. The popular 'Bully's' restaurant, on the other hand, has been there for only three years, although there has been a restaurant on the premises for twenty. It started as 'La Chaumiere' and then 'El Castro'. The present name, incidentally, comes from the proprietor whose name is Bullimore.

To the long-time residents of Llandaff, it will always be 'Pickard's', café, sweet and newspaper shop, but for the past ten years it has been 'The Summer Palace', a Cantonese restaurant which has built up a considerable reputation for providing first-class Chinese food. A remark made recently to a resident was 'You live in Llandaff? Isn't that the place where there's that splendid Chinese restaurant?'

Above: John Williams is a new arrival as a Llandaff High Street estate agent, although he has been in Llandaff for over twenty years. House prices in Llandaff range from £45,000 for a one-bedroom flat, to £450,000.

Left: John Hilling, in his book, *Cardiff and the Valleys*, calls the Probate Registry 'one o the unsung glories of Cardiff's architecture' and 'an object lesson in the harmonious us of materials'. No longer a Probate Registry, it is now the head office of Burnett Davies, consultant surveyors and valuers. When th change of use was approved by the Council four years ago there was some concern expressed that an attempt would be made, despite the status of the building, to make some alterations, especially to the windows, to make it more commercially desirable. This, we are pleased to say, has not happened and we trust that Burnett Davies are happy in their head office.

On the corner of Waungron Road and Ely Road there is an interesting group of shops. Yes, there is an estate agent—Hern & Crabtree—but there is also a general store, a wool shop, a post office/stationers, a unisex hair salon, a fruit and flower shop, a hardware and plant shop and that comparative rarity, a butcher's.

As well as Ruby's takeaway, the shops on the corner of Waungron Road and Fairwater Grove West include Golden Locks Hairstyles, Anthony Russell, Cleaners and a newsagent/video rental shop. Before the Spar began its video rental section, this was the only place to rent videos in Llandaff. Renting home videos began in the 1970s, reached its peak in the mid-1980s and now, mainly due to the quantity of films available by satellite, cable and digital, trade has declined somewhat. Today, people who rent videos, the proprietor says, are usually in the thirty to fifty age group, the young preferring to go out to the cinema and the old to stick to free television and the radio. The man crossing the road with a measuring wheel is probably assessing the width of the carriageway for future roadworks.

Above: Paul Davis who, with his wife Susan, owns the West Grove Stores in Fairwater Grove West. Its main customers are local residents and school children from Cantonian High School and the Bishop of Llandaff School. The most popular items in this stationers, sweet, tobacco, off-licence and general stores are, according to the proprietor, cigarettes, which make up over a third of sales (presumably not to school children).

Left: This small single-storey building, 17 Fairwater Grove East, squashed between two houses, was originally a butcher's (the base of the window display is still a marble slab), then a greengrocer's, then a bookshop before its present use as a clockmaker and repairer. Mr Roberts has owned it for the past ten years and business is apparently unaffected by supermarketry. 'So far!' adds Mr Roberts cautiously.

A chapter entitled 'Buying and Selling' would not be complete without a reference to banking. There are three banks in Llandaff, all within shouting distance of each other. On the corner of Ely Road and Cardiff Road, opposite the Black Lion, is the most recent bank. It has been there for fifteen years but this year in common with other branches changed its name from the Midland Bank to HSBC.

Barclays Bank, on the other side of Cardiff Road has been in the same spot for twenty-five years.

The National Westminster Bank, in the High Street, has been there for twenty-five years. Both Barclays and the NatWest have cash points outside, and both are located at double-yellow lines, (which, we regret to say are frequently ignored by motorists, especially in the High Street).

Nothing changes as often as commercial premises. Since the photographic survey of Llandaff began in 1997, three of the premises have changed hands, one of them twice. Many of them have felt it necessary or desirable to diversify. Hall's bookshop now gives more space to greeting cards and less to books. Cyril Davies, of Llandaff Radio and Television, has for some time sold all kinds of electric appliances as well as radio and television sets. Llandaff Pharmacy has added on site photograph developing and passport photographs to its main service. Both the Cathedral Cleaners in the High Street and Anthony Russell in Fairwater Grove West repair shoes as well as cleaning and the Insole Butcher's also sells fish.

Can these shops survive in the twenty-first century? The great majority of Llandaff residents admit to doing most of their regular shopping at supermarkets, including some of the shopkeepers. We hope so.

Three

Coming and Going

In a cathedral city the key positions are usually held by people who are there more as a career move than out of affection, though affection probably follows. Bishops come and go, as indeed do deans, headmasters, organists and bank managers, and while their contribution to the community may be durably beneficial, their actual time in post may seem quite brief. On the other hand, Llandaff people have been, at least until the Second World War, a stable and closely integrated community. Of those who responded to our Millennium Survey, 2.66% had lived at their address for more than fifty years, 1.7% for more than sixty. Nearly 60% on the other hand had come within the last fifteen years, ninety-five of these within the last year. The ebb and flow continues, with perhaps half a dozen ageing Llandaff folk still living in the houses where they were born.

What changes they have seen. The most far-reaching, surely, has been the takeover of our little city by the motor vehicle which itself contributes to the population's mobility. While 117 responding households had no car, 861 owned one or more, above the average for Wales as a whole. Llandaff's medieval streets do not lend themselves to the accommodation of motor vehicles, and even those of the Insole estate, built in the 1930s, are too narrow for safe parking on the carriageway. More than 17% of residents with up to three cars have no off-street parking. Frustration is increasingly provoked as emergency services, delivery vehicles, through traffic and residents compete for space.

Britain's love affair with the car must, all environmentally-minded bodies agree, be curtailed and the nation, for its health's sake, be encouraged to use its feet. The Taff Trail provides an agreeable riverside link between Llandaff and the centre of Cardiff for cyclists and courageous walkers. The greatest need, however, is for coming and going to be made easier for people with mobility difficulties of one sort or another. The York Transport Hierarchy, which gives priority in planning to pedestrians and disabled people, has this year been commended to the National Assembly for Wales, who are also being urged to put more money into an integrated public transport system.

Above: The Rt Revd Barry Cennydd Morgan, Bishop of Bangor, moves into Llys Esgob, Llandaff, preparatory to being installed as Bishop of Llandaff on 25 September 1999.

Left: The Very Revd John Rogers, dean and vicar of Llandaff since 1993, prepares to cycle away into retirement at the end of November 1999. A devout and diligent pastor, Dean Rogers, his wife Pam and their twins, Paul and Sarah, will be very much missed in the parish.

One of few Llandaff residents still living in the houses where they were born, Les Brodrick spent much of his working life with E. Roberts of Kingsway, high-class outfitters. Now at the age of seventy-seven, he no longer commutes into Cardiff but enjoys gardening at his own doorstep.

Also living in the house where she was born, Miss Nita Tonkin, now ninety, was a tomboy in her youth and, she claims, captain of the football team which played outside the castle wall. She has been, all her life, a great reader.

43

UWIC students walking between the Llandaff campus and their accommodation at Plas Gwyn, Llantrisant Road. Walking, the most environmentally friendly mode of transport, is second only to driving in importance, accounting for a third of all trips, three times as many as public transport and eight times as many as cycling. Along this path beside the Cathedral School playing fields it is also peaceful and free of traffic fumes.

More contaminated by noise and exhaust fumes is the much-used pelican crossing of Cardiff Road at the gateway to Llandaff Church in Wales Primary School. The reassuring presence of Alec Knight, the lollypop man and veteran of the Russian convoys, mitigates the stress of sharing road space with dense and sometimes impatient motor traffic.

The BBC crèche pauses outside the post office, High Street. Single and double baby buggies are a frequent sight in Llandaff, but problems can arise where there are no footways, as on the Green, or where kerbs are high.

This mother will not be able to squeeze her baby buggy along the footway on Bridge Street in the narrow space left by a thoughtless motorist, but will be forced to turn on to the busy road in order to get past.

A runner on Cardiff Road, passing St Michael's College. Training runs more often take place in the green spaces of Pontcanna and Llandaff fields, on the riverside paths or cross country, up and down the Dean's Steps, but they must sometimes at least begin and end on main roads, and happily the road is clear.

Mrs Elaine Jarboe, from Hobbs, New Mexico, and her helper, Rita Smith. Now in her ninety-first year, Mrs Jarboe has lived in Llandaff for over five years with her daughter, Norma, and keeps in touch with her other three children, her nine grandchildren and seven great-grandchildren in the USA by e-mail to Arizona, Oklahoma and Texas. Coming and going is made difficult for her, as for patients from nearby Rookwood Hospital, by high kerbs, cars parked across ramped kerbs and footway obstruction.

Right: A commuting cyclist, properly helmeted and determined to reach his destination safely. Although cycling is now widely encouraged as being healthy, cheap and non-polluting, cyclists are extremely vulnerable to pressure from those drivers who are unwilling to yield road space, and are sometimes invisible to the drivers of large vehicles. Defined cycle lanes would be their protection, but too often parked cars are occupying the carriageway space which might be allocated.

Below: A learner motorcyclist waiting his chance to pull out from Palace Road into Pencisely Road. In contrast to learners in cars, motorcyclists are not allowed to carry passengers until they have passed their driving test, and may not ride a solo motorcycle with an engine capacity in excess of 125cc.

Danescourt railway station, 1999. One of the two-car diesel trains run by Valley Lines between Cardiff Central and Pontypridd pulls in on its way north. Regular passenger services returned to this part of the Taff Vale Railway on 5 October 1987, when two of the three stations in the area, Danescourt and Fairwater, were opened, to provide a welcome alternative mode of travel for commuters and shoppers.

The third Valley Lines station, Waungron Park, opened shortly after. The recently refurbished train shown here consists of two coaches in which seats are in pairs throughout. Two other types are also in service, having different seating arrangements.

Public transport by road, 1999. The Cardiff bus service has been in a state of uncertainty for some years. Pressure from customers for improvement has met reluctance from the local authority to invest in a service with custom apparently declining as car ownership grows. In the context of Agenda 21, however, government insistence on an integrated public transport system has given impetus to the present reorganization. The Clipper, on the right, is run by Cardiff Bus but is due to be phased out; the left-hand vehicle is a privately run school bus and will not be affected.

A double-decker run by Cardiff Bus, also due to be phased out and replaced by Dennis Dart single-deckers. Llandaff has been well served in the past, in the daytime at least, with two valleys companies supplementing Cardiff Bus services to and from central Cardiff, while through-routes have made it easy to reach the extremities of the capital. Drastic restructuring initiated in the second half of 1999, however, has provoked many complaints and is still on trial.

A VEST vehicle, Pencisely Road, August 1999. Voluntary Emergency Service Transport, a charity run by volunteers within the Community Transport system, was founded in 1972. Its eight vehicles can carry wheelchairs and are available to anyone belonging to an organisation for the disabled. VEST covers any distance, including the continent and, apart from a small subsidy from the local authority, it is dependent on donations for its survival.

A driving lesson in progress on Fairwater Road, August 1999. The British School of Motoring, founded in 1910 (when the speed limit was 20mph) has bases in Cardiff, Bridgend, Newport and Swansea, as well as elsewhere in the country. Learner drivers from various driving schools are a common sight in Llandaff. Pupils of BSM can practice on a driving simulator before going on the road in the school's Vauxhall Corsas, and will usually be ready to take their driving test after a period of instruction equal in hours to one and a half times their age (Government estimate).

Richard Beaumont, of Pendinas Cottage, with his 1972 Fiat 500 'Lily Custard'. He is the thirteenth owner of this particular car, the Italian predecessor of the Mini, which, classed as a Historic Vehicle, is exempt from road tax but carries a disc recording 'nil'. Its price when new was £420.

A random assortment of vehicles at the junction of Bridge Street with Cardiff Road, off-peak, July 1999. On the right is a Mercedes, on the left a Toyota, with a London taxi in the middle. For several years Cardiff Road has carried more traffic than its design load, and at peak times vehicles are bumper to bumper from Llantrisant Road to Penhill. The extension of residential development to green field sites to the north is regularly opposed by the Llandaff Civic Society for this reason.

Roadworks in Pencisely Road, August 1999. Coming and going, whether on foot or by vehicle, is sometimes of necessity inhibited by essential works—in this instance gas infrastructure maintenance—on carriageway and footway. Sight-impaired pedestrians may be put at risk by the frequent positioning of warning notices addressed to drivers but partly or wholly on the footway. As these notices have no colour contrast on their backs they are hard to distinguish. The chequered barriers visible on the extreme left, which are red and white, are clear and safe indicators for all road users.

Llandaff Fields, September 1999. On a fine summer Sunday, the most enjoyable approach to Llandaff is to walk in the sun and shade of the horse chestnut avenue and the tranquillity of a vehicle-free environment. Protected by the organization Park Watch from an erosion of the covenant which prohibits development of any kind, Llandaff Fields are a priceless amenity which we hope will long survive for the refreshment of the community.

Four

Palaces and Terraces

'...though the situation of Llandaff is beautiful, and has several elegant residences belonging to dignitaries and other gentlemen, the houses of the poorer people, lying away from the traffic of the main road, and yet collected into a town, have unusually little of that neatness and accommodation which either cleanly retirement, or the more frequent intercourse of society, afford.'

Benjamin Malkin, 1803.

As one looks carefully at the built environment of Llandaff at the end of the twentieth century, it is still possible to trace the stages by which it has changed from the poorly regarded market village of Malkin's day to the prosperous and popular suburb of a capital city.

As with so many places, it was the 'spin-off' effect of the Industrial Revolution which triggered the process of change in Llandaff, primarily through the impetus given by the restoration of the cathedral between 1840 and 1870. Llandaff became perceived as being the place for the 'money-getting' people to live, leading to the construction of a number of grand houses such as Rookwood, Ely Court (Insole Court), Baynton House and Brynderwen. The thatched cottages were demolished or revamped and new, more elegant, houses sprang up on the Green and in High Street and Cardiff Road.

Expansion on to 'green-field' sites brought about such residential developments as Palace Road and Palace Avenue with their wealth of interesting architectural detailing, but it was the inter-war years which brought about the major provision of new domestic housing within the Llandaff boundary. Much of the grounds of Insole Court became Insole Estate with the sale of their land by the Insole family when the construction of Western Avenue cut across it.

The practice of reducing the size of estates, or even the gardens of the more substantial houses, to provide land for building, accelerated in the years following the Second World War, as did the even more recent move into the building of blocks of flats, culminating with The Crescent.

Refurbishment, in the form of replacement windows and roofs, the renewal of cavity-wall tie bars, and extensive modernization, went on throughout the 1990s. Increasingly, families who felt that they needed more room extended their existing homes, rather than move to a larger house for the few years which would pass before the children went off to college. The roof space was a prime target for this expansion of living space either by the construction of 'dormers' or the introduction of a number of roof lights.

So the village of Malkin's day remains only in Llandaff's road pattern and in a few isolated buildings, and the visitor's perception of the place has changed out of all recognition.

Much of 'old Llandaff' was demolished and replaced with new building as the status and prosperity of the village rose in the nineteenth century. This row of cottages, Somerset Place (6 to 14 Bridge Street), came perilously close to demolition immediately after the Second World War but was reprieved and refurbished thus helping to retain the village feeling. More recently some roofs have been renewed and replacement windows have started to appear in place of the original sashes.

Llandaff Court was built between 1744 and 1746 as a residence for Admiral Mathew, who disliked it intensely and never lived there. It was a private house, the Bishop's Palace—Llys Esgob—until the outbreak of the Second World War, when it was requisitioned by the Military. It was also used as a temporary home for the "bombed-out" St Michael's Theological College while its old premises were being restored after the war; it is now the home of the Cathedral School. This is but one example of building recycling in Llandaff, with 'Rookwood', formerly the home of Sir Edward Stock-Hill MP having become a Ministry of Pensions Hospital immediately after the First World War.

Above: Chapel Street, in the heart of Llandaff, is named for the Methodist chapel which is now the Llandaff parish hall. The introduction of a variety of wall colourings and extensive refurbishment has much enhanced the appearance of this nineteenth-century street.

Right: Other large houses which date from the heady days of nineteenth-century industrial expansion, such as Baynton House and Brynderwen, were demolished in recent years as they became too large to be family homes. The fate of Insole Court, originally Ely Court (seen here) long hung in the balance, but concerted intervention by the local community which combined to form an action group helped to save this valuable resource as a centre for leisure and for local activities.

Above: As with other large houses, Insole Court had 'lodges' at its north and south entrances. The South Lodge was demolished in the 1930s while the North Lodge, in Fairwater Road, survived, albeit falling into an advanced state of dereliction as the fate of the main house continued to be undecided. Its fortunes then changed, with major restoration and substantial extension saving it from total loss and converting it into a large and attractive residence.

Opposite below: The lodge to Rookwood also seemed doomed to be demolished, but this charming little building has been restored and extended for use by a department of the hospital.

Right: Cathedral Court was built in 1861-63, to a design by Ewan Christian, as the deanery for Llandaff and served as such until 1953 when it became the Bishop's residence, Llys Esgob. With the construction of a new family house for the Bishop, in 1988, containing purpose-built office accommodation, the old deanery was sold off to be divided into flats.

Below: Cumberland Lodge in Cardiff Road (on the left in this picture) is best remembered as being the childhood home of Roald Dahl, but now forms part of the large music department of Howell's School. The fretted bargeboards of the gables are outstanding and add interest to an otherwise undistinguished Queen Anne style building. Immediately to its right stands the extension to the music department which was built in 1990.

Left: This delightful oriel window and circular turret feature with an extravagant finial is at West Mount in Palace Road. The design gives a feeling of the confidence and prosperity which had now come to Llandaff.

Below: Englemere, in Howells Crescent, is dated to 1914 and reflects, in its exuberant decoration, the sense of stability that was so soon to be shattered in the trenches of France.

Above and below: Palace Avenue (above), and its grander neighbour Palace Road (below), were built in the first quarter of the twentieth century and there was a clear 'Art Nouveau' influence in the choice of decorative features, such as the cast-iron work of this verandah and its sash window detailing in Palace Road.

The building of Western Avenue, as the Cardiff Orbital relief road in the 1930s, led the Insole family to sever their connection with Llandaff and to sell off a large part of their land for building. This naturally became known as Insole Estate, a well-known area with its pleasant, tree lined Avenues and Closes together with its large central grassed area. Bishop's Walk, shown here, is typical of this cohesive development of the inter-war years.

At the head of The Cathedral Green stood Green Court, once the deanery which, with the addition of an extra floor, became the home of the Cathedral School in 1880. When the school transferred to Llandaff Court in 1958, the old school became a derelict blot on the landscape. The site was used in 1979 for what John Newman in his book, Buildings of Wales–Glamorgan describes as 'an attractive and appropriate group of irregularly terraced houses' which were designed by Wyn Thomas & Partners.

As space for new homes in Llandaff, which were demanded in the post Second World War years, became more difficult to find, planners had to resort to 'infilling', using vacant plots such as this example in Pencisely Road.

The Boathouse on Radyr Court Road is built on the sloping lower portion of the divided garden of a house which, although it also faces the river, is technically in Highfields.

Above: This terrace of three-storied family houses in Ely Road predated the construction of Western Avenue and has been comprehensively refurbished in 1998-99 for use as flats. The area in front of these houses was occupied in earlier years by compact and private gardens, now long lost to car parking spaces.

Opposite below: A phenomenon of the later years of the twentieth century has been the replacement of the metal cavity wall ties in many residential properties. Here, in Fairwater Grove West, the work has been completed but awaits redecoration.

Right: A substantial number of houses in Llandaff, as elsewhere, have been enlarged by building an additional room, or rooms, within the loft space. This has been achieved either by using a number of large roof lights and containing the extension within the volume of the roof space, or by extending the roof-line with dormers of which some are more aesthetically pleasing than others.

Below: The extension (right), in St Michael's Road, is lit purely by skylights while the one pictured below, in Prospect Drive, extends the total roof volume.

Former open spaces, such as the playing field of Rookwood Hospital, have been sold off by public bodies to be built upon. The field which was used for games, archery and the annual Rookwood fête is now a close of luxury dwellings named Llandaff Chase.

The largest housing development of recent years was The Crescent, built in 1984-85 on a small field between Mill Lane and Western Avenue. It dominates the prospect of the cathedral from Llandaff Fields, but undoubtedly provides fine views for its residents.

Five

Bread and Butter

Llandaff today contains comparatively few people who both live and work locally. For many people, therefore, 'going to work' involves at least some travelling, possibly into the middle of Cardiff, and enduring the contradictory comforts and discomforts of road transport or the local train service. At the same time the larger employers such as the BBC, the medical and teaching professions and the service industries draw workers of all kinds into the area.

The shops and banks, not only in the High Street, but also those serving the Insole Estate area at Waungron Road and those in or near Fairwater Grove, are staffed by a mixture of local residents and those who come into Llandaff each working day. Similarly, colleges and schools receive their quotas of lecturers, teachers and technicians, together with students of all ages from those at the most junior level to those receiving vocational training from all areas. Administrators and head teachers are also associated with these various centres of learning, together with the caretakers, cleaners and canteen staff who contribute to the well-being of all those in their various institutions. Road crossing patrols brave the ever heavier traffic in Cardiff Road and on Western Avenue, as well as the weather, several times each day so that scholars can cross in safety.

Rookwood Hospital's doctors, pharmacists, physiotherapists and many others continue to care for their patients, and the daily patterns of shift changes see a constant change-over of staff. At the BBC too, employees come and go. Broadcasters, engineers and production staff compile the programmes which we are invited to enjoy in sound or vision throughout all hours of the day and night. The BBC National Orchestra of Wales rehearses, broadcasts and records, with the pantechnicon which ferries their instruments and their music around Wales–and beyond–resting in its parking lot at the end of yet another successful expedition.

The Church in Wales is a good example of an employer operating on more than one site as it employs those such as the clergy, vergers and a secretary on the staff at the cathedral. The warden and lecturers together with support staff work at St Michael's College, and the office staff at the Diocesan board of Finance in Heol Fair. In addition the Provincial offices of the Church in Wales in Cathedral Road employ a number of people who live in Llandaff.

At the close of the twentieth century the concept of Sunday as a non-working day has largely disappeared with goods and services being available to all at any time. Llandaff is not different from the country at large.

In recent years the drive to reduce the vast amount of water lost through leaks in the distribution network, coupled with pressure to improve the quality of the domestic water supply, has lead to a major program of work to renew the old mains pipe work with modern materials. In this photograph a contractor replaces an old lead water pipe to a house with blue polyethylene piping.

Re-lining old cast-iron gas mains with yellow polyethylene piping in Pencisely Road which has had a long history of gas leaks.

Right: A telecom engineer at work at a distribution cabinet for domestic customers' lines.

Below: The collection and disposal of rubbish is an essential part of the work of the Environment Protection Department of the City and County of Cardiff. Here the black bags of refuse, collected from both sides of Pencisely Road, are being thrown into the collection vehicle.

Above: Douglas Longstaffe, the head virger, posts a notice on the west door of the cathedral announcing the closure of the cathedral on the day during which the Electoral College of the Church in Wales was meeting in the nave to elect a successor to Bishop Roy Davies.

Left: Michael Hoeg, the assistant cathedral organist, at the console of the cathedral organ, practising his Sunday voluntary.

Opposite above: The Revd Dr John Holdsworth, the principal of St Michael's Theological College, at his desk in the college.

Opposite below: Supper time at St Michael's Theological College, and the catering staff serve the students in the college refectory.

Above: The 'lollipop-man', a school crossing patrolman, Mr Alec Knight, braves heavy peak-time traffic in Cardiff Road to ensure safe passage for both parents and children.

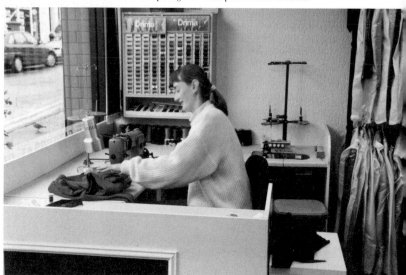

Above: Mr Stephen Howorth and two members of his staff pause for a moment in the course of another working day at the busy chemist's shop, Llandaff Pharmacy.

Right: Perhaps a sign of the times, here outside the Spar supermarket stands Alan Rees offering his copies of The Big Issue to passers-by in the High Street.

Opposite below: If your skirt needs shortening or perhaps a replacement trouser pocket is required, then nimble fingers employed at the Cathedral Cleaners may do those awkward little jobs for you!

Above: The nave of the cathedral presents an attractive setting for the recording or transmission of concerts and recitals. Here a cameraman checks his shooting script prior to the recording of a programme of music for Easter.

Left: Allan Duggan, a prosthetic technician working for Blatchford's at the Artificial Limb Appliance Centre (ALAC) at Rookwood Hospital, prepares a prosthesis for one of the patients attending the centre.

Right: Mrs Jan Wright vacuuming the corridor leading to 'The Den' at Rookwood Hospital. This is an informal area with a children's corner, half-sized billiard table and plenty of easy chairs set aside for patients and their visitors away from the bustle of the wards.

Below: The gardens in front of Insole Court house are enjoyed by visitors and locals alike. Here a gardener tidies the edges of one of the flowerbeds on the lower lawn in early summer.

Left: With bills and cheques, football pools and love letters, circulars and ad-mail, the postman brings the mail to our letter boxes day-by-day, rain or shine.

Below: Nick James, an architectural historian, working on details of the restoration of Ewenny Priory at his drawing board in the offices of Caroe and Partners which are in the newly built Jenkins Court off High Street. This Court is named after the owner of the garage which long stood on the site.

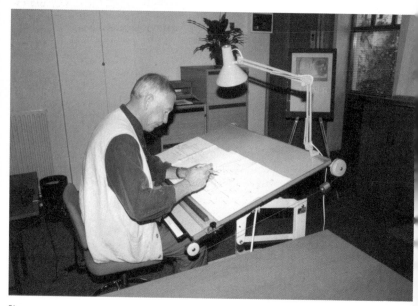

Six

Grouses and Grumbles

The Llandaff Civic Society Millennium Survey asked participants, among other things, to list what they considered were the worst aspects of living in Llandaff towards the end of the twentieth century. By far the most frequently cited was the amount of traffic on our roads, particularly those roads carrying traffic each day into the city centre either from outside the city or from the outlying housing developments beyond Llandaff. An almost inescapable conclusion was that new estates had been sanctioned without any regard to the amount of traffic which was inevitably generated.

Parking too was frequently seen as a legitimate complaint, not only adding to the congestion on already busy roads, but also deterring many from shopping in the High Street. The abuse of the 'yellow line' system was repeatedly remarked upon, as was the practice of unloading from excessively large goods vehicles, effectively blocking the road at its narrowest point. People whose cars had been vandalized, often repeatedly, in the car park in the very centre of Llandaff felt that the installation of surveillance cameras could bring about a great improvement in the situation.

Other sources of complaint were the condition of the roads themselves and the prevalence of litter. Overflowing rubbish bins and the inefficiency of the newer motorized road sweepers when compared with the 'old fashioned' man, brush-and-barrow system were felt to lead to a build-up of rubbish in corners and other places beyond the reach of the vehicles. The riverbanks also came in for their share of criticism as looking sadly neglected and strewn with litter.

Sometimes it was the built environment which troubled our respondents. The BT telephone exchange on Western Avenue was seen as overpowering and totally inappropriate in its position, where perhaps screening with trees might have softened its impact.

Parents of young children bemoaned the lack of safe play areas near to their homes, especially as many modern houses have gardens too small for boisterous young children. Facilities for teenagers were also felt to be inadequate, leading to opportunities, temptation and involvement in vandalism and other anti-social behaviour.

A few people living on the Insole Estate adjacent to the junior school deplored the closure of the pathway through the school grounds, which caused great inconvenience to more elderly people who wished to use the shops in High Street. The converse view regarding the peace of mind of the parents of pupils at the school was also expressed.

A heartfelt grumble concerned the closure of the public library in Insole Court. This was seen as the removal of a much valued facility, other branch libraries in the city being inconveniently placed for many, particularly those households which had no private transport. It was the loss of a much cherished social amenity.

A typical view of the traffic in the mornings when the line of vehicles passing through Llandaff towards Cardiff is unbroken. The flow of traffic is further delayed by no less than six sets of traffic lights between the junction with Fairwater Road and the Penhill crossroads. In the evening, of course, the flow is reversed and many respondents to the Llandaff Survey said that the heavy traffic and the associated fumes were what they most disliked about living in the area.

When the Spar supermarket first opened, it was understood that all goods would be unloaded through the large parking area behind the shop. Today, the increased size of delivery vehicles means that this is no longer possible and, as a result, High Street is congested with heavy vehicles discharging goods immediately opposite the access to the public car park—even crossing the road becomes a hazardous operation.

A number of respondents remarked upon the problem of driving on roads already congested with parked vehicles, particularly in High Street and Fairwater Grove West where difficulties arise when vehicles going in opposite directions wish to pass. This 'on-road' parking often occurs either where public parking areas are not perceived to be safe or where access to private parking through narrow back lanes is difficult. The modern car is generally considerably larger, as well as more powerful, than its counterpart of earlier years.

Graffiti seem to appear overnight and to last for a lifetime! They frequently act as a magnet to attract other 'artists' to wield their spray cans in contrasting colours. Only quick and thorough removal will discourage this form of vandalism.

Above: Litter always defaces our surroundings and when large items, possibly left out in a fit of optimism with the weekly 'black bag' for collection, remain untouched, the results are particularly to be deplored. The existence of special arrangements for the collection of bulky items needs better publicity linked with firm enforcement of 'anti-litter' bye-laws. Access to the 'green bag' recycling scheme would also be very welcome.

Above: When the Taff is in flood the resulting flotsam of paper and plastic is left to litter the bushes along its banks until a special cleanup operation can be mounted, often much later. However, the dropping of food and drinks containers such as this soft drink can seems to occur at any time and in every public place.

Left: Junk mail is one of the householder's constant irritants. This is one week's collection of free newspapers and advertisements which came through one letter box in Llandaff. Little of it is likely to be read or even be of interest, and all of it has to be disposed of—more waste of materials.

Opposite Below: A number of people felt that litter bins were emptied too infrequently so that, as is seen here on the Cathedral Green, carelessly dumped rubbish, often seemingly brought into the area, is left to blow around the place.

Opposite above: As part of the aftermath of the shooting tragedy at Dunblane, security at our schools has become of prime concern to parents, teachers and governors alike. No longer can anyone use the Llandaff Primary School grounds as a short-cut to the village centre, and the gates are kept firmly locked. This is a source of some friction with good arguments being advanced by both camps

Left: The four-storey extension to the telephone exchange was felt by a number of people to be totally out of scale and lacking in sympathy with its immediate surroundings, together with a singularly unfortunate choice of materials.

Below: Parents ask where their children can play safely close to home, but here in the open space between Insole Groves East and West this notice makes it very clear that only children who are ten years of age or younger are permitted to play there. Of course, young children would require constant parental supervision since this grassy area is entirely surrounded by roads.

The Playing of Ball Games in This Area by Children Over the Age of 10 is Prohibited

Below: The closure of the branch library at Insole Court was cited by many respondents to the Llandaff Survey as being, in their opinion, the worst thing about the place. It was felt that a valuable social asset enjoyed by people of all ages had been removed. For many people, too, a visit to another branch or to the central library posed practical problems both in terms of the weight of books to be carried and in the poor availability of public transport. The 'Friends of Insole Court' have attempted to redress this loss by opening, once a month, in one part of the building, a coffee shop and book morning from shelves stocked with donated books of all kinds.

Despite its apparent air of tranquillity, this public car park which serves the centre of Llandaff has an appalling history of car crime. This deters motorists from using it other than at peak times so that their attempts to park in less vulnerable situations only seem to add to the existing problems of congestion.

These are but some of the things about which people felt concern when they answered the questionnaire, but often what some saw as a problem – such as the proximity of Llandaff to Cardiff or the number of public houses – others saw as a virtue. Other 'worst things' such as 'un-neighbourliness' simply defied pictorial illustration in a way which could be included in this book. Even more were, as would be expected, an expression of a particular personal view very sincerely held by the respondent.

Seven

Flora and Fauna

This must be a celebration of what we have and enjoy rather than of what we have lost. The venerable London Plane on the Green is probably the senior survivor, and is the haunt of owls by night and jackdaws or wood pigeons by day. Junior partners, ready to inherit, have been planted at a distance on either side. Beeches, especially copper beeches, and the cedars of Lebanon at Insole Court and Llandaff Place dwarf present day planting of rowan, birch and cherry, and we are lucky to have mature Turkey oaks in Llandaff Fields and the splendid horse chestnut avenues there and at Insole Court. There are several gingkos in older gardens; the Indian bean tree shelters a well-placed bench near the Old House, and in the spring a white blaze of magnolia lines Palace Road and neighbouring corners. Dean's Wood is mainly beech, and the wooded walk to the river from Pontcanna Fields mainly lime. How precious, as the traffic thunders past UWIC on the A48, are the mature limes originally belonging to the Marquess of Bute. By contrast, the oak avenue, planted in 1989 across the Arls field, has established itself pretty well in spite of vandalism, one gap having been filled by a seedling grown from an acorn found in the crop of a pheasant run over by a member of the Society a few years ago.

In the 1980s the Cockpit in Llandaff Fields was reclaimed by the Society from use as a rubbish tip after the Second World War and made an area for environmental studies; eighty-eight plant species were identified there in a single day. Along the riverbank invasive Japanese Knotweed is taking over from its rival, Himalayan Balsam and native species such as ox-eye daisy, even piercing tarmac in urban locations. The modest Mexican fleabane, however, and blue fleabane, also thriving in Llandaff, can be welcomed without reservation.

As for local wildlife, grey squirrels, bats and hedgehogs are common, foxes, rabbits and mink have been seen and in certain places frogs and toads are tenderly nurtured. A mute swan's egg was discovered in the Cathedral south churchyard in 1998, but probably originated elsewhere.

Observations of butterflies found a marked decline between 1997 and 1999, especially in small tortoiseshells and red admirals; meadow browns, the commonest in 1997, were far fewer in 1999. Speckled woods were still common. Similarly one must record the conspicuous decline in garden birds from previous years noted by our observers in 1997. Watching fifty-nine locations in the area, however, our observers managed to log seventy-seven species including dipper, firecrest, goosander, whitethroat and cuckoo, as well as all familiar garden birds, still there for the birdwatcher who knows where to look and listen.

Ffordd Gerallt, an oak avenue across the Arls field. Planted in 1989 by the children of Llandaff schools under the guidance of Forest of Cardiff, this follows the course of a broad tree-lined road shown on Speed's map of 1610 leading from Llandaff Cathedral to the River Taff.

Monterey cypress (*cupressus macrocarpa*) in the north, transpontine graveyard, one of the survivors from John Prichard's original planting in 1860.

Seeds of Wych elm (*Ulmus glabra*), in Spring 1999, growing in the boundary hedge of the Victorian graveyard. The Wych Elm appears to have a greater resistance to Dutch elm disease than the common elm, which, from being a prominent feature of the British landscape, has now been almost annihilated.

Photographed in the snow in April 1999 on the wall dividing 'Town & Country' from the Llandaff Institute, Maidenhair Spleenwort (*Asplenium trichomares*) with in the left-hand clump Hartstongue (*Phyllitis [Asplenium] scolopendrium*) and on the right just visible Wall-rue (*Asplenium ruta-murania*). These three ferns which grow in walls are indicators of a damp atmosphere.

The primrose (*Primula vulgaris*) photographed in March 1999 in the churchyard. These early blooms are also found on the riverbanks and in many gardens.

Wild arum, Lords and Ladies, Wake Robin, Cuckoo pint (*Arum maculatum*) found in March 1999 by the Dean's Steps and in Dean's Wood along Ffordd y Meirw and elsewhere. The purple spike within its pale green spathe develops a basal group of poisonous green berries ripening in July to a brilliant red.

Wood anemone or Wind Flower (*Anemone nemorosa*) photographed in March 1999 in the transpontine graveyard.

Japanese knotweed (*Reynoutria japonica*), an established alien first conspicuous in the Llandaff area after the Second World War and now superabundant.

Above: A mass of Lady's Smock—Milkmaid—or Cuckoo Flower (*Cardamine pratensis*) growing in a damp meadow beside the Taff. This meadow resulted from the building in the 1980s of the flood protection bank which runs from Western Avenue to Llandaff weir.

Left: Himalayan Balsam (*Impatiens gladulifera*) photographed in October 1999 in the Arls field where it grows abundantly. Himalayan Balsam spread along the course of the mill stream after the Second World War. The flowers vary in colour from white to the deepest rose pink and have a heavy scent.

Mexican Fleabane (*Erigeron karvinskianus*) photographed in summer 1998; an invading species noticeably increasing on the congenial stones of Llandaff. This can no longer be described, as it was in the 1970s, as rare.

The North American Blue Fleabane (*Erigeron philadelphicus*) photographed in late September 1999 outside Pendinas on the Green.

Above: A male blackbird, a regular visitor to a Pencisely Road bird table. Adaptable and prepared to eat a wide variety of seeds, fruit and berries, as well as snails and insects, blackbirds have been the great survivors in the decline of garden birds noted in recent years. Our 1997 survey logged 3,140 observations, the maximum on one occasion was 29; comparative figures for the song thrush were 383 observations.

Left: A female blackbird with unusually light breast plumage. This bird was a regular and partially tame visitor to a Llandaff bird table until August 1999.

Right: Two adult greenfinches, and a juvenile, taking nuts from a feeder in a Llandaff garden. The total sightings of greenfinches were 1,052, with an average of 3. This species has kept up well in the average garden, particularly when the correct food, such as sun flower, especially black sun flower, and finch mixture is provided.

Below: A juvenile lesser black-backed gull begging for food from an impassive adult, September 1999. Lesser black-backed gulls were first observed nesting in the high chimneys of Llandaff in the early 1960s, and from Spring to August they now have a common and opportunistic presence. A migratory species, only individuals which have established hospitable food sources stay beyond August. Most go south, though possibly no further than Steepholm.

Jackdaws foraging on the Green, September 1999. Flocking more densely in winter, this community is often seen circling the Prichard tower or roosting in the beeches of Dean's Wood. The most seen at one time was 48.

A mute swan's egg, with hen's egg for comparison. Found in the south churchyard in 1998, the egg, which was addled, may have been laid there and abandoned, but is more likely to have been transported by human agency.

Two common wasps approaching the entrance to their nest in a garden shed in August 1999.

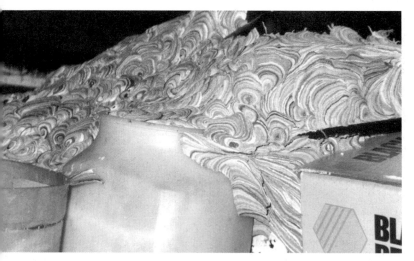

The nest of the common wasp (*Vespula vulgaris*) inside the shed. Begun by the queen wasp on emerging from hibernation in the Spring, the nest is made of chewed wood pulp which hardens into paper and each cell contains an egg which hatches into a worker wasp. By August the community, feeding on insects, has grown to its maximum size, and eggs which will produce new queens and also male wasps are laid. The new queens leave the nest, mate with the males and disperse; the nest is ultimately deserted and will not be used again.

Above: The common frog, September 1999. The (nationally dwindling) frog population is encouraged in some Llandaff garden ponds, where frogspawn appears in early February and tadpoles mature by June. Frogs which survive return for hibernation either in the mud on the pond bottom or in some dark damp corner of the garden.

Left: A fox (*Vulpes vulpes*), surprised in daytime on a Pencisely Road garage rooftop, 1998. Seldom seen in daylight, foxes have in recent years frequently been observed in and around Dean's Wood at night, on the Insole Estate and railways embankments. The dog's bark and the vixen's scream are heard in the mating season. They scavenge for food in litter bins round the cathedral, leaving unsightly debris.

Eight

Sports and Pastimes

The century which has just passed has seen enormous changes in the way we spend our leisure time, including of course, the amount of time now available for leisure. This chapter is mainly concerned with group activities, but, unsurprisingly, more people who answered the Llandaff Society questionnaire admitted to liking sport as a spectator rather than as a participant, which probably meant home television viewing. That their numbers will continue to grow is the fervent wish of those investors in digital, satellite and cable television.

Where pastimes are concerned, major sporting events, pop concerts and festivals are attracting greater numbers than ever before, while at the same time more people listen to music in the seclusion of their private earphones and play solitary computer games at home. Both are handled by major commercial interests. Will they replace or diminish the smaller local sports and pastimes? They could, if we don't watch out.

Unlike its near neighbours, Ely and Fairwater, Llandaff has no leisure centre. There used to be an open-air swimming bath at the corner of Llandaff Fields, but it was closed some years ago, and in the 1990s it was demolished, the area filled in and grassed over. What Llandaff does have is Llandaff Fields, an area of about seventy-one acres which, since 1898, by a deed of covenant, can only be used for recreational purposes. It provides a number of rugby football pitches, pitches for cricket, hockey and baseball, tennis courts, a bowling green and a children's playground. What are not provided are adequate changing facilities, the present building leaving much to be desired, and apparently there are no plans for any improvement in the foreseeable future. Nevertheless Llandaff Fields is a delightful and important social amenity, and we should be grateful especially to the Thompson family of Whitley Batch, who were largely instrumental in ensuring that it remains unchanged.

The playing fields on the other side of Western Avenue from Llandaff Fields, are where the team of Llandaff Rugby Club play when at home and where the matches of the Llandaff Cricket Club are held. And then there is the River Taff, home of the Llandaff Rowing Club. Sport is not badly catered for in Llandaff.

Since the closure of the Memorial Hall, off the High Street, and its conversion to a 'Jazzy Jungle' play area for the under tens, Llandaff has no hall suitable for amateur drama or concerts available to the general public. The parish hall next door is too small, and even Insole Court—ideal for some events—can only accommodate an audience of about seventy with any degree of comfort. This is probably the reason why many events tend to be held in the open-air, on the Green, in the gardens of Insole Court and, sometimes, in the Old Bishop's Palace.

A visitor to Llandaff arriving on Twelfth Night, Shrove Tuesday, the day of the summer Rainbow Fair, or the night of Hallowe'en might well believe that the Twelfth Night revels and the Hallowe'en Games at Insole Court, and the Pancake Race and Rainbow Fair on the Green were events with a long tradition. In fact they are all comparatively recent events or revivals, and demonstrate that Llandaff still has a village community spirit—and enjoys it.

The flourishing Llandaff Rugby Club was formed in 1876 at the instigation, it is believed, of Sir Illtyd Thomas, who lived locally. One of the first clubs in the Welsh Rugby Union, Llandaff has always endeavoured to be in the forefront of developments in Rugby, and was one of the first to organize youth rugby in Wales.

A few years after the Rugby Club was formed a rowing club on the Taff came into existence. It was called The Taff Rowing Club, a title which was changed to The Cardiff Rowing Club, becoming the Llandaff Rowing Club in 1946. Today, with three hundred members, it is one of the largest in the country. It is often stated that, 'It always rains on Regatta Day', but in 1999 this was clearly an exception.

Above: The clubhouse of the Llandaff Rugby Club is now named 'Llandaff Rugby and Athletics Club'. Among other activities, every Thursday at 7p.m. a group of about forty members take part in an hour's run. Six of these were photographed at 8p.m. [some still smiling]. They are, left to right: Eddie Amblin, Elaine Adams, Carolyn Llewellyn, Jeff Aston, Dave Roberts, Dave Wilkins.

Right: The Llandaff Cricket Cup is a recent addition to Llandaff's sporting life. It was formed in 1998, the teams for the first draw being the Heathcock, the Black Lion, the BBC Club, Churchill's Hotel, the Maltsters Arms, the Rowing Club, the Llandaff Rugby Club and the Butchers Arms. In 1998 the Black Lion team was the winner, and the cup (left) was proudly displayed in the saloon bar. In 1999 the BBC National Orchestra of Wales won the cup.

During most weekends Llandaff Fields is well-used for football (both association and rugby union) baseball, tennis and bowls. The well-established bowling club (founded in 1932) is seen here play the team from Taff's Well.

It was the idea of one of Llandaff Fields' County Rangers, Catherine Healey, to organize a new k of activity in the field—worm charming. The idea is to collect worms from the ground by any mea short of digging—jumping, dancing or beating the ground, even playing a musical instrument. In 1998 the day selected for the first event was a rainy one, and few people turned up. The day for next year's charming was windy but dry, and seventeen eventually participated, and seemed to enj it. It could catch on.

Right: Mention needs to be made of the largest pastime of all—television watching. Nothing specially Llandavian in that, of course, even though BBC Cymru Wales has its headquarters here in Llantrisant Road.

Below: And where sport is concerned the pubs and clubs have turned television into a community pastime. After all, if you can't get into the match itself, watching it in a convivial atmosphere must be the next best thing. And Llandaff Institute was a good place for members and guests to watch the Rugby Worl Cup Final on Saturday 6 November—even if Wales was not playing!

Left: A pancake race on Shrove Tuesday is a part of an ancient and elaborate custom at Westminster School. Here by the Green, Llandaff's races are more straightforward and of recent origin, but just as enjoyable an event. Sprinting up to the War Memorial, heats are divided into age groups, including one for the mothers. One of the two young runners seen here appears to have lost or forgotten his pancake.

Below: Another annual event which takes place on the Green is the Rainbow Fair, held on a Friday evening in summer. The Green is closed to traffic, stalls are set up by a number of local organizations and a brass band play. Popcorn and hot-dogs are consumed, games are played, there is a children's fancy dress competition and for a few hours Llandaff really feels like a village, rather than a part of Cardiff. The fair was the brainchild of the Very Revd Alun Davies when he was dean and vicar of Llandaff.

Professor and Mrs B. Hibbard are rightly proud of their garden at the Clock House, Cathedral Close, and have had an Open Day, in association with the National Gardens Scheme, for many years. Each year, Professor Hibbard says, when he thinks of the amount of preparation involved, it is going to be the last time.

As the sign above the main entrance says, the Llandaff Institute was founded in 1866. Up to the outbreak of the Second World War it was also the headquarters of Llandaff Rugby Club, all its members being members of the Institute as well. Today there are over 450 members.

One of the places for sporting types to meet is the Maltsters Arms. There is no golf course in Llandaff, apart from a miniature course on Llandaff Fields, but the Maltsters Arms is the headquarters of the Dragons Golf Society, and a glass case of trophies in the bar bears witness to this. Their cricket team has made it to the final, both in 1998 and 1999.

The Scout Hut, off Cardiff Road, is not only used by Scouts. It is also used by Cubs, and those at pre-Cub age, (between six and eight years) the Beavers.

Above and below: Insole Court, the nearest building Llandaff has to a stately home, is a valuable community centre. Among the activities during the day are Joyce Frazer's Yoga class (held on Thursday mornings from 10 a.m. to noon) and lessons in embroidery.

Above: When the Friends of Insole Court decided to mark Hallowe'en by organizing an early evening of appropriate games for children under ten, including the traditional bobbing and ducking for apples and dressing up as witches, ghosts and vampires etc., they were surprised to discover that some schools declined to advertise the event because it was regarded as a celebration of a pagan festival and therefore anti-Christian. There was no problem about an evening of carols and wassail, arranged by the Council with the help of the Friends. In 1998 this included a modern bit of mummery, with Steve Killick (as Father Christmas) and Dick Berry.

Christmas wouldn't be Christmas in Llandaff without the Handbell ringers.

Nine

Church and State

Since Norman times the four ancient Welsh dioceses, including Llandaff, had been subject to Canterbury. Then, in 1920, they were disestablished and disendowed. The new Church in Wales was free to manage its own affairs through governing and representative bodies, to elect its own bishops and archbishops, and to legislate for itself in matters like liturgical reform. It was no longer the state church, and old enmities between the established and free churches began to die down.

Yet curious anomalies remain. The cathedrals still use the state prayers for the Queen, and on national occasions they are still the focus of worship and celebration. This is most marked at Llandaff, as cathedral of the capital of Wales, and before the inauguration of the Welsh Assembly Her Majesty the Queen attended a service here. Local Christians of all denominations still look to the cathedral as the mother church, the earliest place of Christian worship in the area.

This association in the popular mind was most marked in the outbreak of mourning on the death of Diana, Princess of Wales. The cross was swamped in flowers and gifts brought by individuals. For weeks people queued in the south aisle to sign the Book of Remembrance. Llandaff Cathedral was the venue for the Welsh national service of remembrance held at the same time as the funeral of the Princess in Westminster Abbey, which was relayed to the nave and outside on the Green on huge television screens.

There are many services attended by seafarers and members of the armed forces, whose memorials are in the cathedral. Each year the judges come in solemn procession before the Cardiff Assize.

Llandaff Ward elects two local councillors, and is part of the wider constituencies which elect an MP to Westminster and a delegate to the National Assembly. Though the local police station has closed, the community policeman and traffic wardens are as familiar on our streets as the robed clergy going about the business of the parish. Llandaff remains a centre for diocesan, provincial, and civic occasions, and the affairs of church and state continue in an unofficial partnership.

Left and below: During the Victorian restoration of the cathedral a sequence of sovereigns' heads was carved along the south aisle wall head, culminating in the uncrowned head of Edward VIII. Despite the 'Llandaff Legend', which foretold disaster either for Cathedral or monarchy when the south side was filled, both continue to flourish, as witnessed by this carving of the head of Queen Elizabeth II by John Excell of Clarke's of Llandaff. She and her father George VI have taken their place on the north aisle.

Her Majesty the Queen, in the flesh, climbs the Cathedral Hill after the service for the inauguration of the Welsh National Assembly, 26 May 1999. Captain Norman Lloyd-Edwards, Lord Lieutenant, is in attendance. In the background the Duke of Edinburgh chats with the schoolchildren.

Prince Andrew, Duke of York, is the royal guest at a Seafarers Service. He greets the crowd at the same spot, accompanied by Captain Lloyd-Edwards, appropriately in naval uniform.

Above: Arriving for the National Assembly service is the local Member of Parliament and Assembly Member, Rhodri Morgan. He is accompanied by his wife Julie Morgan MP for the neighbouring constituency, and Sue Essex AM.

Left: Anxious to associate themselves in the public mind with the concerns of the locality, candidates in the local election in May 1999 are photographed against the background of the cathedral.

Right: Public mourning at the sudden death of Diana, Princess of Wales, focused on the cross at Llandaff, with offerings of flowers, toys and messages of sympathy. On 31 August 1999, two years afterwards, flowers were still being laid here to mark the anniversary. In the background, shepherded by their choir master and organist, Dr Michael Smith, the boys of the cathedral choir are on their way to practise for the memorial service.

Below: On the Green a giant television screen relays the funeral service of the Princess from Westminster Abbey. Another screen was provided in the cathedral for the congregation at the national memorial service for Wales, taking place simultaneously.

The Dean, Very Revd John Rogers, welcomes the South Korean ambassador and civic dignitaries to the service of dedication of the memorial to those who died in the Korean conflict in the Welch Regimental Chapel.

Shenkin, mascot of the 2nd Battalion, The Royal Regiment of Wales (24th/41st Foot), joins the welcome with his Goat Major, Cpl David Joseph BEM.

Above: Llandaff parishioners and pupils from the Cathedral School gather for the laying of wreaths at the War Memorial on Remembrance Sunday. Revd Matthew Tomlinson, priest vicar, conducts the service. In the statuary by William Goscombe John (who himself once sang in the cathedral choir) a workman and a schoolboy stand either side of a symbolic female figure, Llandaff bidding farewell to her children.

Right: The community policeman, DC Darren Jones-Matthias, is on a normal day's duty alongside the War Memorial.

Above and left: Policing in the British tradition? A friendly chat with a former Lord Mayor of Cardiff, Councillor Max Philips (above) and (left) mingling with the crowd at the Rainbow Fair on the Green.

Right: John Harrison, traffic warden, though courteous, may be a less welcome representative of authority as he goes about his work in the High Street.

Below: The Lord Chief Justice arrives for the annual legal service which draws another specialist congregation to the cathedral.

Left: Representatives of different Christian denominations arrive at the cathedral for the installation of a new Bishop of Llandaff, 25 September 1999. Revd John Garland and Revd Gethyn Abraham-Williams, representatives of the Free Churches, are followed by the Most Revd John Ward, Roman Catholic Archbishop of Cardiff.

Below: Rt Revd Barry Morgan greets the spectators before his induction and installation as Bishop of Llandaff. He is preceded by the Chancellor of the Diocese, Judge Norman Francis, and followed by his chaplains including, on the left, Revd Frank Price.

Above and right: Following the custom of his predecessors, the new Bishop knocks on the door of the cathedral and is admitted by the Dean, the Very Revd John Rogers.

For the Bishop's installation, the nave of the cathedral is filled to capacity. The congregation includes representatives of every aspect of the life of the area—clerical and lay, civic and national, educational, legal, commercial—in a setting which mingles the architecture of Norman, medieval, Victorian and modern times. Sir Jacob Epstein's great statue of Christ in Majesty presides over the latest episode in the story of church and state.

Ten

Facts and Figures

Benjamin Disraeli, who might well have had a passing acquaintance with Llandaff when he is said to have lodged at the 'Cow and Snuffers' in Llandaff North, is credited with the pronouncement that 'There are three kinds of lies: lies, damned lies, and statistics'.

When the Llandaff Society, as part of its Millennium programme, set out to provide future generations with a picture of how our community lived in the closing years of the twentieth century, it decided to ask every household in the Parish of Llandaff, and, with the welcome aid of their Residents' Association, in the newer community of Danescourt, to provide answers to a series of questions which do not appear in the ten-yearly national census. Some of these questions called for 'factual' replies while others sought opinions.

In sending out the questionnaire the Society was very aware that, in general, the response rate to what many people might regard as 'junk mail' is notoriously low so there was considerable relief when, out of the 2,259 households in Llandaff, 992 (43.9%) replied. The response from Danescourt was almost as good with 403 questionnaires (32.8%) out of the 1,227 delivered being returned. Respondents had been assured that the information which they had supplied would be confidential, so each returned questionnaire was allocated a serial number before the answers were analyzed to ensure that anonymity was preserved. No list exists which could link these serial numbers to such names and addresses as have been supplied.

With such a high level of response the picture of our communities which emerges from the replies is reasonably representative of the total population and gives some very valuable information. It is also of great interest to compare the old and established community of Llandaff with the comparatively new community of Danescourt.

The Llandaff Society's sincere thanks go out to all those people who took the time and care to reply to this survey.

The information in this chapter must, however, be treated with due caution as, in the words of Samuel Johnson, 'Round numbers are always false', but with the source material safely held in the Glamorgan Record Office, future researchers will be able to produce their own assessments of life in Llandaff at the close of the twentieth century with a perspective that only the passage of time can give.

The pupils of Ysgol Pencae helping with the task of preparing the Llandaff Society Millennium Questionnaires prior to delivery supervised by deputy head teacher Mrs Sylvia Price.

The houses in which we live. These houses in Waungron Road are typical. Over three quarters of our homes are a mixture of brick and stone, are three-bedroomed and have front gardens with off-street parking for at least one car. Of all properties, 54% already have replacement windows and half have roofs of coloured tiles—many of them replacements of slate or pottery tile roofs.

Hardwicke Court, built on the site formerly occupied by Brynderwen, the home of the David Morgan family. 24% of our housing stock in Llandaff consists of detached houses with four or more bedrooms. 10% have five or more bedrooms. By contrast 40% of the homes in Danescourt are detached, but with less than three percent having more than four bedrooms.

Parking congestion on the Cathedral Green on a Sunday morning. The twentieth century love affair with the internal combustion engine is reflected in the pattern of car ownership. Half of all households in Llandaff owned one car, one third had two cars, 4% had three cars while about 1% had four or more cars. Only 12% of households had no car. Multiplying up our sample to represent the whole population of Llandaff suggests that there are almost 3,000 cars 'resident' in Llandaff! It is significant that 16.3% of households have no 'off-street' parking facilities. In Danescourt, built in the age of the car, less than 3% of households have no off-street parking, with less than 6% having no car—half the rate in Llandaff!

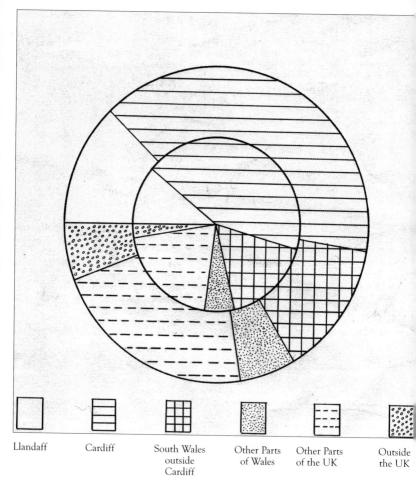

Llandaff	Cardiff	South Wales outside Cardiff	Other Parts of Wales	Other Parts of the UK	Outside the UK

Where do we come from? This pie chart summarizes peoples' replies as to where they were born. When this information is combined with information about how long families have lived in their present home, it gives a picture of increased population mobility at the end of the twentieth century. The outer ring refers to Llandaff, while the inner ring shows the proportions for Danescourt.

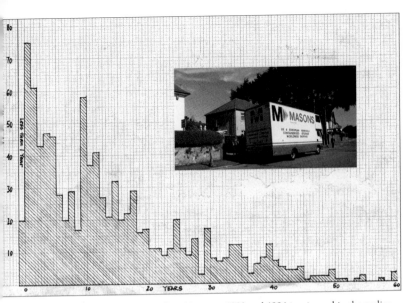

Years in the present house: The 'turn-down' between 1989 and 1994 is mirrored in the replies from Danescourt and would seem to be related to the national economic cycle. Seventeen replies were from people who had lived in the same house in Llandaff for over sixty years and two had stayed put for over seventy-five years.

A summer's afternoon on the terrace of Insole Court. It is in population profile that Llandaff and Danescourt most differ, as one might expect when comparing an old community with a comparatively recent development. The under-eighteen age group in Llandaff accounts for just over 19% of people while in Danescourt the figure is a shade over 26%. The working population (18 to 65) account for nearly 59% of Llandaff people whereas nearly 65% of Danescourt residents fall within this age band. It is in the 'pensioner' category that the greatest disparity appears—22% in Llandaff compared with a mere 9% in Danescourt.

Of the population of Llandaff, 11.9% claim to be Welsh-speaking compared with 7.6% in Danescourt. 'Mill House' on Western Avenue was built, as its name suggests, as a residence for the miller of Llandaff Mill. After the demolition of the mill in the 1930s to make way for the construction of Western Avenue, it served as a private house, as part of the headquarters of the short-lived television company WWN (Wales West & North) and more recently as part of the offices of the Welsh Joint Education Committee.

Above: Information about the use of computers in homes is changing more rapidly than any other of the facts which appeared in the survey and already our figures are out of date. Nevertheless, the state of play in 1998 is worthy of being recorded, showing as it does the differences between Llandaff and Danescourt, which are most likely due to the different age structures of these two communities. In Llandaff 45% of households owned a computer of which 13% were connected to the Internet while in Danescourt 53% of households had machines with over 18% being on the Net. It will be interesting to look back on these figures in ten years time! Here John Vesey interrogates the Cathedral Belfry website on the Internet.

Right: The Preaching Cross is central to the village and stands not just for the 'Cathedral' form of worship but for the Christian faith in general to which 41% of our population claim allegiance. A further 9% subscribe to other faiths.

Above: Spencer's Terrace, opening out behind the archway into Spencer's Row, with its sense of privacy and quiet immediately gives a feeling of a 'village'. The things which people most disliked in Llandaff have been well aired in the chapter on 'Grouses and Grumbles' but there were almost as many aspects of life in Llandaff which appealed to residents as there were replies to the Millennium survey. Above all the answers reflected the way in which the 'village atmosphere' (28%) and 'the environment in general' (25.5%) was of prime importance.

Opposite below: The parks and open spaces such as Insole Court and Llandaff Fields are most valued (11%) as are the opportunities afforded for walking.

Right: Whether one attends its services or not, Llandaff Cathedral is central to the physical structure of the village, and rates highly in many people's regard for the place (22.4%).

Below: 'Proximity to Cardiff' was favourably noted in 14.5% of replies while 'ease of transport' was remarked upon by only 8% of our respondents. This photograph of the centre of the city, dominated by the newly completed Millennium Stadium, is taken from the top of the Jasper Tower of the cathedral looking to Cardiff across Llandaff Fields.

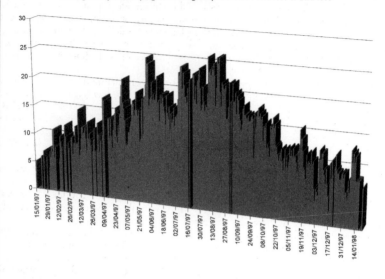

Average Temperature (Degrees Centigrade) - Llandaff - 15/1/1997 to 21/1/1998

One of the incidental pieces of information to emerge from the bird survey was a day-by-day measurement of temperature taken by one of the bird recorders. This may well be a very interesting set of data in future years if predictions of global warming come to pass.

THE LLANDAFF MILLENNIAL HOUSEHOLD

The typical Llandaff household at the close of the Millennium appears to consist of 2.38 people who have lived for less than twelve years in their present home, which is a brick built three-bedroomed semi-detached house with replacement windows and a roof of coloured tiles. They have 1.32 cars upon which they rely as their main means of transport and for which they have off-street parking space. As a result only some of the household shopping is done in Llandaff with most of it outside the village.

The head of the household is probably a full-time teacher, administrator or manager, or is involved in medicine or engineering. Unemployment stands at just over 5%. Except for present-day pupils, it is unlikely that any of the household were educated in Llandaff, and most were probably born in Cardiff or other parts of South Wales rather than in Llandaff–although 27% of the population of Llandaff were born outside Wales. Over 40% of the households came to Llandaff, because of marriage or for family reasons, with 27% coming because of employment.

The typical household will, most likely, not have any pets, is unlikely to take part in leisure classes or watch sport, although one in five might participate in sporting activities– 'Entertainment' and 'Home based activities' are the major spare time activities. Almost half the households will have personal computers but only a fifth will have a modem and only one in nine will be connected to the Internet.

Forty per cent of people claim to attend some place of worship (although the degree of regularity is not known) while only 22% are involved in any form of voluntary work.

The great majority of households sit down to their main meal in the evening but eating either with friends or in a restaurant is only an 'occasional' event. The traditional 'meat and two veg' figures as the favourite dish (20%) with half as many families opting for fish (11%). Pasta comes in third at 7.1%. Only 6.4% of households put any form of poultry as their first choice. Over 63% of respondents admit to being alcohol users.

They, almost without exception, rate traffic in its various guises as being the worst thing about Llandaff. But nevertheless it is generally viewed as a pleasant, convenient place to live with high marks for its friendly, 'village' atmosphere, its access to open spaces, its proximity to Cardiff and the sense of 'place' engendered by the Cathedral and by Insole Court.

Acknowledgements

The Llandaff Civic Society welcomes this opportunity to record its gratitude to the many individuals and organisations who have helped us with our millennium project. In particular we thank: Dr Matthew Griffiths, Civic Trust for Wales; Dr Liz Hughes, University of Wales, Aberystwyth; Chris Rhodes and Gaynor Williams, RSPB; Heather and Robert Henderson, Cardiff Naturalists Society; Geraint Talfan Davies and Margaret Bird, Controller and Senior Producer Education BBC Cymru Wales; Lady Trotman-Dickenson, Welsh Heritage Schools Initiative; Llandaff Rotary Club; Brains Brewery; Blackwell's; Danescourt Residents' Association; the Millennium Experience; Cardiff City and County Council; Llandaff Cathedral Archives; the Friends of Llandaff Cathedral; Llandaff Labour Party; Howell's School; Peter Leech; David Lewis; William Clarke, and many more. We are grateful to COLAB for their unstinting assistance throughout the project. The contribution of Dan Langford and Sarah Young of UWIC has been incalculable.

We congratulate David Samuel, winner of the Video Competition, 'My Llandaff'. We also congratulate the children of Ysgol Pencae and Howell's Junior School who entered our competition, especially the prizewinners, Medyr Llewelyn and Kimberley Lloyd-Owen, and those highly commended, Tanwen Berrington, Rosie Meek, Alice Patillo and Rachel Simpson.

The Llandaff 2000 team of photographers comprised: David Abbott, John Bethell, Norman Cunningham, Nevil James, John King, John Lewis and Regina Smith. The following members of the Llandaff Society worked on the compilation of this book: Norman Cunningham, Lisbeth David, Chrystal Davies, Jill & Nevil James. Matthew Williams was good enough to write the introduction, Arwyn Lloyd Hughes to read the proofs, and Jane Friel of TEMPUS gave us help and advice.

Our members and friends have given generously in time and other resources throughout the seven years since 1993, especially the seventeen who put together the 3,850 questionnaire packs and the forty members who delivered them, and this was much appreciated. Special thanks are due to John Bethell, who has chaired the Steering Group from the beginning.